MW00625724

LA DOLCE VITA
CIGARS

To: JAKE

ENJOY !

NH
NEW
HOLLAND

FORREST

First published in 1999 by
New Holland Publishers (UK) Ltd
London • Cape Town • Sydney • Auckland

24 Nutford Place
London W1H 6DQ
United Kingdom

80 McKenzie Street
Cape Town 8001
South Africa

Level 1, Unit 4, 14 Aquatic Drive
Frenchs Forest, NSW 2086
Australia

Unit 1A, 218 Lake Road
Northcote
Auckland
New Zealand

10 9 8 7 6 5 4 3 2 1

Copyright © 1999 New Holland Publishers (UK) Ltd

ISBN 1 85974 157 6

DESIGNED AND EDITED BY
Complete Editions Ltd
40 Castelnau
London SW13 9RU

DESIGNER: Blackjacks
EDITORIAL DIRECTION: Yvonne McFarlane

Reproduction by PICA Colour Separation, Singapore
Printed and bound in Singapore by Tien Wah Press Pte Ltd

Picture Credits: The publishers would like to thank Cigars Unlimited, the Modernism Gallery,
San Francisco, *Cigar Aficionado* magazine, Rêmy Martin Fine Champagne Cognac, Cuba
Tourist Services, the Library of Congress, Washington, D.C., Asprey and Garrard Ltd, *Cigar
Style* magazine, Cigar Connoisseur, Frank Spooner Picture Library, Imagebank/M Regime,
Tor Imports, N. R. Silverstone Ltd, The Cigar Club, Grapharchive and the Corcoran Collec-
tion. Cover photograph by George Wieser, Jr. Permission granted by Black Dog & Leventhal
Publishers, Inc. © 1996 Black Dog & Leventhal Publishers, Inc. Every effort has been made to
identify other illustrations. Any errors or omissions will be corrected in future editions.

CONTENTS

FROM SIK'AR TO CIGAR

The Story of the Cigar

> *"He twirled a gay guitar*
> *He smoked the sweetest cigar.*
> *He lay in the grass*
> *With the head of the class*
> *And left her all ajar."*

M.L. ROSENTHAL, *BLUE BOY ON SKATES*

Cigar-smoking has always had a mystique, an air of panache and style. Today this is is as strong as it has ever been, with cigar bars and glossy cigar magazines attracting new cigar-smokers of both sexes worldwide to the pleasure of smoking a good, big cigar.

The Spanish were the first Europeans to sample this delight. The day Christopher Columbus first landed in Cuba, 28 October 1492, he noted in his log that the local Indians, both male and female, smoked a "lighted brand from which they inhaled."

History shows that Indians in Central America and the Caribbean had been enjoying these forerunners of the modern cigar long before Columbus arrived.

Carvings on a 2000-year-old temple in Mexico show a Maya priest puffing at a tubular roll of leaves. And the Spanish word *cigarro* comes from *sik'ar*, the Mayan word for "smoking".

The Cubans encountered by Columbus's party called the plant they smoked *cohiba*, a name which has been handed down to become the brand of one of the most sought-after Havana cigars in Castro's Cuba.

By 1520 the plant, and the practice of smoking it, had reached Europe. A century later smoking had become so widespread in Europe and the Middle East that many rulers took steps to curb it. In 1614, King James I dealt a serious blow to smoking in Britain when he wrote his infamous treatise, *A Counterblast Against Tobacco*.

A decade later, Pope Urban I forbade Spanish priests to smoke cigars. To top everything, the great 1650 fire of Moscow was conveniently blamed on a recalcitrant cigar-smoker.

However, official disapproval did little to stem the growing enthusiasm for smoking.

From the start, the Spanish were the creators of the cigar industry. The famous Seville Royal Factories were founded in 1731. In 1831, King Ferdinand of Spain granted Cubans the right to produce and sell tobacco on the island, which was still a Spanish colony.

Cuba was soon overrun by cigar-makers, largely supplying the Spanish Crown. To this day, the island, even under Fidel Castro, annually sends a symbolic batch of *cohibas* to the King of Spain. And Spain returns the compliment by being the world's largest importer of Cuban cigars.

Juan
Pablo II

¡Bendícenos!
21 al 25 de
Enero de 1998

*Enjoying a Havana
during the Pope's visit
to Cuba in 1998*

AND HAV
TRADE

ANAS EMBARGOES

(*Cigars in America*)

Tobacco plants imported from Cuba and Central America, were cultivated in the British colonies of North America from the late 1600s, though the first crops were intended for use in pipes, the British manner of tobacco-smoking.

American smokers got a taste for cigars in the second half of the 18th century. After the colonists won their independence from Britain in 1783, cigar factories sprang up in Connecticut, Pennsylvania and New York State.

A big conglomeration of factories developed in Conestoga, Pennsylvania, hence the American slang for a cigar, a "stogie".

Cigar-smoking in America reached a peak after the Civil War, with American companies

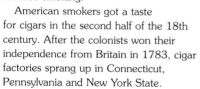

"Our country has plenty of good five-cent cigars, but the trouble is they charge fifteen cents for them."

WILL ROGERS

making cigars from a mixture of Havana and home-grown tobacco leaves.

As with other luxuries, such as coffee, which gave sustenance to revolutionary thinkers, and whisky, which was heavily involved in Scottish politics in the 18th century, so cigars have their place in history.

The Cuban writer and revolutionary José Martí liberated Cuba from Spanish rule in 1895-6 with the help of the thousands of cigar-makers who had fled to Florida. The plans for the rebellion were sent from Key West to Havana rolled in a cigar. Thank goodness no-one lit up.

Sixty years later, Fidel Castro's supporters delivered messages to him while he was briefly imprisoned on the Isle of Pines, hidden in his allowance of cigars.

Once Castro had gained power in Cuba, in 1959, a failed attempt to overthrow his socialist regime indirectly dealt a severe blow to US cigar-smokers.

Backed by the US government and armed by the CIA, a force of Cuban exiles

made an unsuccessful attempt in April 1961 to invade Cuba at the Bay of Pigs, in the south of the island.

President Kennedy, newly elected to the White House, looked for another way of toppling Castro and placed an embargo on all US trade with Cuba.

However, the Cuban economy was not the only victim of his action. The import of all cigars from Cuba into the USA was banned, along with the rest of the island's exports. With the benefit of prior knowledge, Kennedy did his best to ensure his own well-being. Summoning his press secretary into the Oval Office, he told him, "I need a lot of cigars. About a thousand. Call all your friends and get as many as you can."

Pierre Salinger found 1,100. JFK thanked him and produced the Cuban trade ban legislation from his desk. He said, "Now I can sign this!"

This ban is still in force, though US Customs' legislation does allow American cigar-smokers to import a limited quantity of Cuban cigars "for their own use"!

Seated on a high chair, a lector reads aloud to entertain cigar-rollers in 19th-century Cuba

ROLLED GOLD

(*Making Cigars*)

A cigar has three main components. The filler as the name suggests, forms the innards of the cigar. In premium brands these are long, folded or pleated leaves, running the length of the cigar, which allow free passage of air along its entire length.

Less expensive brands can be filled with chopped up leaves, shaped into a filler.

The filler is held together by the binder. These two components are then covered by the wrapper, a whole leaf of best quality, chosen for looks, feel, and potential aroma. This is what you see when you first choose your cigar.

"In a hectic world cigars give people a chance for a pause. It's a ritual."

MICHAEL DOUGLAS

The cap, a round shape cut from a leaf, is then stuck in place on the end with a spot of vegetable gum.

Most premium cigars are rolled by hand, with only a wooden mould to help create the perfect shape. Others are completely machine-made. Often there is a combination of the two processes. The filler and binder can be machine-prepared, with the finishing touch, the wrapper, being applied by hand. This enables the roller to take out the thick vein of the wrapper leaf; completely machine-made cigars often have too many veins on the wrapper.

The band is applied before the cigars are bundled or boxed.

The traditional design and labelling of cigar boxes started in the 1830s when H. Upmann, the banking house in London and Havana, named after its founder, Herman Upmann, shipped Cuban cigars to its London office in sealed cedar boxes stamped with the bank's emblem.

For the specialist there are also bundles of fifty cigars, like those being prepared in the picture above, tied with ribbon and packed in plain square cedar boxes, known as the Cabinet Selection.

In 1837, Ramon Allones, a cigar-maker who had emigrated to Cuba from Spain, began making the cigars that have borne his name ever since. He is also credited with being the first to put coloured labels on his boxes.

For those who like their cigars "green", H. Upmann introduced airtight glass jars to keep them fresh and moist.

Individual cigars are often found in aluminium tubes, which not only maintain their moist condition, but also prevent damage or contamination.

For a true aficionado, though, there is only one way to keep cigars in perfect condition – in a humidor.

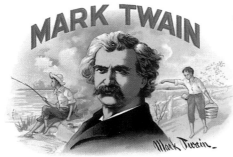

"If I cannot smoke cigars in Heaven, I shall not go."

MARK TWAIN

Cigars have to be stored carefully, in the cigar shop, in the tobacconist, or at home.

It is essential that cigars should not dry out. So, when buying cigars, it is best to avoid the ones displayed in open boxes on shelves – unless the open boxes are in a humidor, that is.

The perfect humidor is a good-sized room at your favourite cigar supplier. Dimly lit, maintained at a regular temperature and, most importantly, with consistent humidity, these are the ideal conditions in which to make your first encounter with the cigar of your choice.

(One tip, when visiting a humidor, is to avoid wearing strong perfume or aftershave. The controlled conditions of the humidor will cause their aromas to linger and affect your sense of smell when choosing your cigar. For the same reason you should never smoke in a humidor.)

HUMIDOR
HEA

16 LA DOLCE VITA

Few of us have a spare room at home to set aside as a humidor like this and portable humidors will do the job of maintaining the condition of our cigars just as well.

These range in size from those that will humidify a handful of cigars, to those which can accommodate an entire collection.

Many humidors, both traditional and contemporary, are exquisite works of art. In London, the Chelsea firm of Cigars Unlimited specialize in bespoke, hand-crafted design to produce exotic humidors that are destined to become the antiques of the future.

Some of the unique humidors created by the designers and craftsmen of Cigars Unlimited

Hand-made humidors in this league command high prices. At an auction in Havana in 1998, £40,000 (US$64,000) was paid for a cedar and mahogany humidor modelled on a tobacco-curing barn – but it did contain 100 Vegas Robaina cigars.

This price was topped by the £65,000 (US$104,000) paid for a Trinidad humidor. Made of cedar and sterling silver, this was engraved with views of Trinidad and contained 101 Trinidad Dunadorues (Havana cigars, despite their name), together with a silver cigar cutter inlaid with gold and ivory.

It was signed by Fidel Castro.

CLARO, COLORADO, OR OSCURO

> "When finally getting to the British Open those fancy London tobacco shops were a whole new world of forbidden fruit."

TOM WATSON, CHAMPION US GOLFER

First find your cigar merchant, for part of the enjoyment of cigars is the almost sensual ritual of choosing and buying them. This is particularly so if you find an establishment with a humidor, where you can savour the cigars to the full.

Discriminating cigar-smokers take the same care in choosing their cigars as they do in making the other great pleasurable decisions of life.

Although there are enough brands and sizes to satisfy anyone's needs, be adventurous, for there are cigars which suit some circumstances and events better than others: small cigars for minor occasions, or to satisfy an urge at home; large cigars for great occasions, or solitary contemplation after a good dinner to accompany a favourite brandy.

Cigars are not to be smoked like a hurried cigarette. They must be enjoyed in a leisurely atmosphere and appreciated like the finest wine or foie gras.

Cigars are not for satisfying an addiction to tobacco. They offer delights to the eye and the nose, to the palate and to the sense of touch. Concentrate on these and you come to understand why cigars have held a special appeal for approaching 500 years.

The first consideration when choosing your cigar is its appearance. It should look as well tailored as the prospective smoker. Smooth, regular in shape, with an even girth that should feel firm to the fingers.

The colour of cigars ranges from the lightest, almost blond, known as Claro, and Colorado Claro which has a tawny hue,

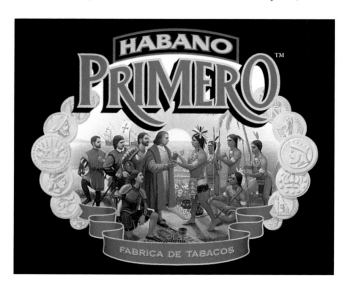

to Colorado which is a reddish dark brown, and Colorado
Madura which is a true dark brown made from the most mature
tobacco leaves.

There are regional variations within these main categories, often
specially created for a particular market, such as the Oscuro from
Nicaragua, Brazil and Mexico, which is virtually black.

*The elaborate
art of the
cigar-box label*

SIZING UP CIGARS

R 3/8"typ

1/4" Cap

7"

There's a cigar size for every aficionado and occasion, from a small cigarillo to a double corona.

Confusingly, different manufacturers haphazardly interpret the sizes in their own way. This is not a precise science.

CIGARILLO: the smallest up to 6 inches (15 mm) and no bigger than 29 ring (see diagram). Good for a quick ten-minute fix.

PANATELLA: Long and narrow, from 5 to 7 inches (12.5 to 17.75 mm), with a ring size up to a 39. A slightly longer, quick fix.

CORONA/PETIT CORONA: Stubbier than a panatella, with a ring size of 40 to 44. They provide a fuller smoke, say a generous half-hour.

LONG CORONA/LONSDALE: Just over 6 inches (15 mm) with a ring of 40 to 44. Named after the Earl of Lonsdale who

> *"The nipple [his cigar] was coffee-coloured and six-inches long."*
> ALDOUS HUXLEY, *TIME MUST HAVE A STOP*

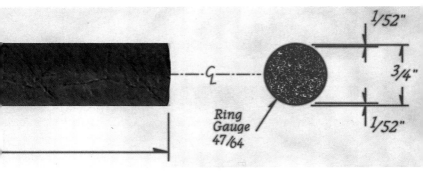

Ring Gauge 47/64

1/52"

3/4"

1/52"

commissioned a Havana factory to produce his own distinctive style, in the early 1900s. The box bears his portrait.

GIANT/GRAND CORONA: Longer than a Lonsdale, but often with a small ring, around 44. You can get a good hour out of one of these.

ROBUSTO/TORO: Another size of squat cigar, packing a kick into a small package. They deliver the fullness of their longer cousins, in half the smoking time. Around 6 inches (15 mm) and with a ring anything from 48 to 54. Often called a Rothschild, after the financier Leopold de Rothschild, for whom they were created by Hoyo de Monterrey, so that he could enjoy a rich flavour without the time-consuming effort of a longer cigar.

CHURCHILL/DOUBLE CORONA: The longest and fattest, the king of cigars, measuring 7 inches (17.75 mm) and upwards with a ring ranging from 46 to 54. Put a generous hour aside to savour this one.

RITUALS
AND

Having chosen your cigar, now is the
time to truly luxuriate, but not
before a certain amount of ritual
has been observed.

First is "Off with its head!" The closed end
of the cigar has to be opened to allow the
smoke through. Biting it off is a favourite
practice of detectives in Raymond Chandler
novels, but there are more elegant and
effective means. Aim high and buy a good,
razor sharp cutter in an elegant case if you
want to achieve a good, clean, straight cut.

Cheaper models can produce uneven ends
or "drag" the tobacco. You can use an
extremely sharp pocket knife if you are
sure-handed. You need only cut about one-
sixteenth of an inch (1.6 mm) off to give you
a good burn and even draw.

Piercing the closed end with a match, or
even with a specially manufactured tool, is to

RITES

be avoided as it tends to draw the smoke
and oils of the tobacco down onto the
tongue. Most disagreeable.

In days gone by, particularly when
offered a cigar in a restaurant, the cigar
was warmed along its whole length.
This practice began with the cigars
produced at factories in Seville. The
wrappers were stuck on with a gum which
affected the taste of the cigar when lit.
Nowadays the pinhead of vegetable gum
used to fix the wrappers is completely
odourless and tasteless.

The question of whether and when to
remove the band is a moot point. Some
say the band was originally placed on cigars
to protect the fingers of gentlemen's gloves
from tobacco stains. At one time removing
it was *de rigueur* in Britain, though not so
necessary in many other countries. Today,
many regard removing the band as non-U.

If you do decide to remove it, take great
care. It is all too easy to crack the wrapper.
Press the cigar gently below the band and
ease it off with dedicated care.

The Swiss cigar expert, Zino Davidoff,
advises that the band should only be
removed when the cigar is at "cruising
temperature", roughly when one-fifth has
been smoked and the body of the cigar has
shrunk just enough to facilitate removing
the band.

Light your cigar with a wooden match or spill, or a gas lighter. Do not use sulphur or wax matches, or a petrol lighter, as they will affect the flavour. There are specially made lighters for cigars, produced by Colibri, Dunhill and others. As gift items they often incorporate a cutter.

And once ignited, enjoy! Take good even draws, filling your mouth with smoke. Retain it briefly and then let it out. Cigar smoke is not meant to be inhaled. The sensation of the immensely satisfying taste of the smoke in the mouth is sufficient.

Some cigarette-smokers find this difficult at first, but a lungful of cigar smoke will suggest that savouring the smoke in the mouth is much more pleasing. This is not to say that the occasional tiny inhalation cannot be enjoyable.

If, for some reason, your cigar goes out when part-smoked, and leaving it in an ashtray for a few moments too long can cause this, do not worry about re-lighting it. Once this was regarded as infradig,

but now everyone does it. Make sure the end is even, sometimes the wrapper is longer than the filler. You can burn off the ragged edges before re-lighting carefully to ensure an even burn.

Finally, there is no need to grind a cigar in an ashtray when you finish smoking. Leave it in the ashtray and it will die with dignity of its own account.

In Victorian times, cigars were an essential part of the lengthy multi-course meals which were enjoyed by the upper classes, often being kept lit throughout the evening.

A hearty Baron of Beef immediately suggests itself as suitable partner to a good cigar. Choose a rich, aromatic cigar, with a deep brown wrapper.

Game is a natural with cigars, even rough ones with full-flavoured wrappers. A sweet cigar is particularly suitable to accompany savoury game stews and pies.

Seafood does not appear to be a natural cigar companion, but it is remarkable how spicy seafood and Creole dishes can match up with a strong cigar. Equally, a smooth cigar, such as a Dominican, can enhance the flavour of lobster and other shellfish.

And then there are always glorious truffles. Total decadence.

(Eating and Drinking)

CIGAR
COMPANIONS

Alcohol is the most natural ally of the cigar. Fine wines appear fruitier and smoother when enhanced by an equally fruity and smooth cigar, such as those from Honduras and Nicaragua.

Port is eternally linked with the post-prandial brandy. Buy the best of both for the perfect pairing. A vintage port from one of the great houses, such as Graham, Cockburn, Sandeman or Fonseca, to name a few, slip down the throat silkily when paired with a full-bodied cigar with a rich brown wrapper.

Cognac and Armagnac again demand a full-flavoured Dominican or Honduran cigar. If you can find it, there is the El Sublimado cigar, which is lightly flavoured with 50-year old cognac. Similarly, the El Incomparable cigar is flavoured with a single malt Scotch. The Scotch of your choice works well with lighter cigars.

Americans swear that any cigar goes with any Bourbon, especially as a late-night pairing before a late-night pairing. Classic Bourbons such as Wild Turkey and Jack Daniels are now joined by specialist Bourbons such as Knob Creek and Maker's Mark, which are not readily available at every outlet. They match the greatest cigars.

If you are of non-alcoholic persuasion, and few dedicated cigar smokers are, try a cup of one of the smoky China teas such as Lapsang Souchong or Gunpowder, now universally available. Cheers!

"Until you've had a good cigar and a shot of whisky, you're missin' out on the second and third best things in life."

ALAN J. LERNER, *PAINT YOUR WAGON*

CIGAR
SEÑORITAS

"A woman is only a woman,
but a good cigar is a smoke."
RUDYARD KIPLING

Cigar-smoking is seriously back in fashion. Cigar clubs are opening worldwide and cigar magazines go from strength to strength. Many leaders of the market are women. At the George Sand clubs in Santa Monica and Manhattan, two-thirds of the members are women.

In showbusiness, Madonna wielded a Churchill (maker unknown) on the prime-time David Letterman US television show – largely to upstage her host. Whoopi Goldberg, who started on cheap cigars as a child, now sports Cohibas. Supermodel Linda Evangelista has appeared on the cover of *Cigar Aficionado*, another Cohiba fan. But she is reported as saying that she can't go the whole way.

Nicole Kidman and Tom Cruise travel with a humidor.

The raffish, 19th-century, French writer George Sand was probably the most famous female cigar-smoker, closely followed by Liszt's mistress, who wrote under the name Daniel Stern. And then there is Bizet's heroine, Carmen, who enjoys a cigar (for cigarettes were not common then) in the city square.

In America, Bonnie Parker, poetess and bank robber (along with Clyde) smoked cigars, as did Marlene Dietrich and her friend, Ernest

Cigars used to promote Rémy Martin cognac

Hemingway, who sent Ava Gardner the band from the cigar he was smoking the night they first met. The French novelist, Colette, also partook of Havanas.

Today's trend is actually a return to what was once the status quo; it was not until the mid-19th century that cigar-smoking became a male prerogative.

In 1735, an English traveller in Costa Rica wrote of ". . . leaves of tobacco which are rolled in such a manner that they are the pipe

and the tobacco itself. These the ladies, as well as the men, are very fond of smoking."

Since that time, women who smoke cigars were regarded as sexually perverse, indeed it was written that ". . . a woman who smoked a cigar sent a signal that she had assumed the male prerogative of taking pleasure in public. And so cigars became props for women who staged their sexuality in public – gypsies, actresses and prostitutes."

How times change.

Illustration: S. Bornstein

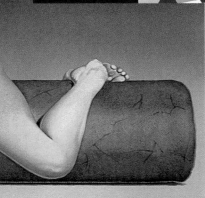

The sexual connotation of the cigar is fairly obvious and, perhaps, adds to its appeal. Mel Ramos's painting Hav-a-Havana, *in the Modernism Gallery, San Francisco*

CIGAR HAVENS

(Bars and Clubs)

Cigar clubs and bars are blossoming on both
sides of the Atlantic. In London's Notting Hill,
Tom Conran, son of cigar-smoking Sir Terence,
runs a pub-restaurant that features special cigar
evenings and has big, big cigars for sale.

The banning of smoking in public places
across America has led to a boom in US cigar
clubs, cigar bars and exotically named divans.
With them has come a host of cigar
publications, led by the mighty *Cigar
Aficionado*, which has a monthly circulation of
750,000. In its pages are listed 650 bars, clubs
and restaurants where cigar lovers can meet
and enthuse over their favourite blend and size.

The magazine also hosts an annual gala
dinner in Havana to which the authorities turn
a blind eye. It costs £250 (US$320) a head, is
strictly black tie and provides the perfect
opportunity to get through fifteen smokes,
while slaking your thirst with as many Mojitos
(a concoction of rum, sugar, lime, mint and
soda water) as you can cope with.

On a more modest level, notable restaurants that welcome cigar lovers include the famous Morton's in Chicago, which boasts the model Lauren Hutton (opposite) and Jack Nicholson amongst its regulars.

Smart New York cigar bars range from the Rainbow Promenade atop the Rockefeller Tower and the Plaza Hotel, to the Havana Cigar House (where you *cannot* get Havanas), the Concierge Cigar Club and Señor Swanky's. There are another forty welcoming cigar-smokers.

Back in Europe, where the attitude to smoking is more liberal, the few cigar clubs that exist have always been for the genuine relish of cigar appreciation, rather than a refuge from virulent anti-smokers, though most restaurants now ask clients to "refrain from pipe- or cigar-smoking".

In London, traditional meeting places like The Little Havana (where you *can* get Havanas, the No 1 Cigar Club, the Bar Cuba and the Havana Club have been joined by recently opened cigar bars. At the end of 1998 Granada Hotels launched cigar bars in three of its flagship hotels: Le Meridien on Piccadilly, the Waldorf and the Grosvenor House.

Wherever you are, it doesn't take long to appreciate that cigar-smoking engenders a much more convivial atmosphere than cigarette-smoking, a camaraderie, a feeling of fellowship that draws you in as the heady aromas permeate the room.

"I owe everything to cigars."
SIR JIMMY SAVILE

Lauren Hutton, a regular diner and cigar-smoker at Morton's in Chicago

ONE PM, SEVERAL PRESIDENTS

The most eminent cigar-smoking politician of this century has to be Winston Churchill, British Prime Minister during the Second World War. He had been a serious cigar-smoker since he first came across them in Cuba, at the age of 22. He smoked ten cigars a day which, it is estimated, means nearly a quarter of a million over his lifetime – he lived until he was 90 years old.

During the war, Cuban companies sent him 5,000 cigars, when shipping was interrupted. The cigar became, along with the victory sign, Churchill's symbol. He is now immortalized through the huge Churchill, manufactured by Romeo y Julieta.

"I only smoke cigars with people I trust."
SADDAM HUSSEIN

AND A COUPLE OF REVOLU

Churchill was as famous for his quick wit and bon mots as he was for his famous radio broadcasts and speeches.

Irritated once by Field Marshall Montgomery, who had pontificated, "I don't drink. I don't smoke. I sleep a great deal. That is why I am 100 per cent on form", Churchill retorted, "I drink a great deal. I sleep little and smoke cigar after cigar. That is why I am 200 per cent on form."

IONARIES

A Churchill has also become a
generic name for a cigar that size
made by other companies.

In America, many presidents have
had intimate relations with "seegars"
or "stogies". George Washington
grew tobacco, but didn't smoke it.
President John Adams and his son,
John Quincy Adams, were serious
smokers. The first incumbent of the
White House was James Madison,
fourth president. He smoked
obsessively, but still lived to be 85. His wife, Dolly, was addicted to
tobacco in a different form – she took snuff.

President Jackson and his wife shared cigars, but President Taylor
had to smoke alone, as cigars made his wife ill. General Grant
smoked ten cigars a day and when it was reported that he was
smoking in the middle of a battle, the public inundated him with
10,000 cigars. His consumption went up. When he ran for
president in 1868 his campaign song was "A Smokin' His Cigar".
Presidents Arthur, Harrison, and McKinley were avid smokers. It
was recorded that the latter was never to be seen without a cigar in
his mouth, except when he ate or slept. Though he did have a
delicate wife and was reduced to chewing half-cigars when with her.

President Taft "the most oval man to inhabit the Oval Office",
enjoyed an occasional cigar, but his successors, Teddy Roosevelt and
Woodrow Wilson, abstained.

However, Wilson's Vice-President, Thomas
Marshall, made cigar history. After listening to a
lengthy speech on "what America needs", he
uttered the immortal line "What America needs
is a good five-cent cigar."

They got it, but made by machines and
fairly nasty.

Presidents Harding, Coolidge and Hoover
carried on the tradition – Coolidge never without
his own big, double corona, but always ready to
accept a gift of another. President Kennedy was
the last serious cigar-smoker, having started as a
young man when his father was American
Ambassador at the Court of St James.

And from then on presidents were either abstemious, smoked pipes or had difficult wives.

President Clinton sports a cigar often when playing golf. But does he inhale? Hillary Rodham Clinton banned tobacco in the White House, but obviously not with complete success as negative publicity surrounding her husband has confirmed.

On the other side of the political spectrum, cigars became the hallmark of Fidel Castro and Che Guevara (who overlooks the bundling of cigars opposite) as they planned their revolution and emerged from their mountain fastnesses to overthrow the Batista regime in Cuba.

Cigar lover, President Clinton, enjoying two of his favourite pastimes

CIGARMANIA

Cigars loom large in literature and in showbiz. They feature in paintings and caricatures of literary figures ranging from Honoré de Balzac and Stéphane Mallarmé to Henry James and Charles Dickens.

William Makepeace Thackeray enjoyed a good cigar, calling it the "great unbosomer of secrets". In his novel *Vanity Fair*, Becky Sharp loved "the smell of a cigar out of doors . . . and tasted one . . . giving a little puff and a little scream and a little giggle."

The Freudian imagery attributed to the cigar is well

Sigmund Freud, who formulated theories on psychoanalysis and the cigar

earned, as Sigmund Freud himself was an enthusiast; at the turn of the 20th century Freud formulated his theories with friends over weekly cigar-smoking sessions. Before his marriage, Freud said, "Smoking is indispensable if you have nothing to kiss". He thought of the cigar as a symbol of tenacity and self-control.

The cigar has also been a potent dramatic prop for many years. P. T. Barnum presented the midget General Tom Thumb, The Smallest Man in the World, smoking the largest Havana he could find.

Charlie Chaplin used it in silent films to show his sudden wealth. Whilst Laurel and Hardy and Harold Lloyd employed cigars for visual gags. W. C. Fields used a cigar in his role of riverboat captain in *Mississippi*.

At the other end of the spectrum, Bertolt Brecht, author of *The Threepenny Opera*, praised the "cheap cigar" and planned to open an "epic smoke-theatre".

Ernst Lubitsch, Hollywood director, chain-smoked cigars while making such classics as *Ninotchka*. Reputedly, he died in bed with a blonde astride him and a corona still smoking in his ashtray.

Jack Warner was smoking a panatella, made by Hoyo de Monterrey, when he broke the bank at the Cannes Casino, clearing a cool 100 million francs.

> "I smoke in moderation. Only one cigar at a time."
> MARK TWAIN

Darryl Zanuck, creator of *Gone with the Wind*, owned his own plantation in the Vuelta Abajo district of Cuba.

Orson Welles said that he only made films so that he could smoke cigars for free. Other thespians who are keen cigar aficionados range from Clint Eastwood, who made spitting into the desert dust a trademark, to Roger Moore, Pierce Brosnan and Robert de Niro – and, of course, Jack Nicholson. They all prefer Havanas.

And then there are the two cigar classics, George Burns and Groucho Marx, never seen without a cigar in their hand, on stage and off.

George Burns said, "If I'd taken my doctor's advice and stopped smoking, I wouldn't have lived to go to his funeral." He was 98 at the time. Even at 100 he could manage ten cigars a day. As he got more forgetful, the pauses in his act, covered by lengthy puffs on his cigar, became funnier than the script.

Groucho famously said that he wouldn't join a club that would have him as a member. One "club" he was a fervent member of was the international circle of cigar aficionados.

And so to today, when that international circle takes in Colonel Gaddafi and Placido Domingo, Danny de Vito, and Arnie Schwarzenegger, Saddam Hussein and Jack Nicholson. A motley crew, brought together by their love of the great cigar.

Supermodel Eva Herzigova brings the cigar to the international catwalk

TOBACCO TALK

Around the Cigar World

Cigars are made from tobacco grown in a number of countries. This is blended to create variations in taste and aroma. Many countries produce small amounts of tobacco for local use, while others dominate the world market. For beginners in the art of the cigar, it can be helpful to start by trying cigars of a particular country. Because of climatic and soil differences, the cigars produced in one country will have a recognizable characteristic. But this is not an immutable rule.

BRAZIL: Two large regions produce medium and full-bodied tobacco which is used world-wide and widely blended.

CAMEROON: Seeds from tobacco plants in Cameroon are now used worldwide. Their leaves produce strong aromas and are very popular as wrappers.

CUBA: Home of the cigar and producer of the greatest – Havanas. The secret lies in the soil of four regions where superb fillers and wrappers are produced. Often regarded as a heavy tobacco, Cuban tobacco can also be tenderly mild.

DOMINICAN REPUBLIC: Now produces tobacco for most of the world's premium cigars. The long leaves make superior fillers and the Dominican Repulic now produces wrappers as well. The finished cigar is often on the mild side.

ECUADOR: The climate here, almost always cloudy, is ideal for the production of classic mild wrappers, with a subtle taste.

HONDURAS: Tobacco grown in this Central American country is seriously rich and aromatic, making it the runner-up in the premium cigar stakes. Hurricane Mitch caused widespread damage in 1998.

JAMAICA: Jamaica produces mild tobacco. The first Jamaican tobacco was grown by Cubans who fled their island after the revolution of 1898.

MEXICO: Tobacco grown here runs the gamut from wonderfully smooth to quite harsh, which does not necessarily mean bad. Notable binder leaf is grown, as well as pungent *colorado madura* wrappers.

NICARAGUA: War-torn country where the tobacco industry has just about survived. In peaceful times excellent cigars have been produced, often with a sweet after-taste. In 1998 Hurricane Mitch devastated the area.

SUMATRA: Not the widest-known tobacco grower, but substantial amounts of mild wrapper leaves are produced on Sumatra and on neighbouring Java.

UNITED STATES: Folk imagination suggests the Deep South as a major tobacco producer, but in reality the classic leaves are produced in the Connecticut valley. This is perfect shadeleaf used as wrapper for premium cigars.

To sum up, cigars made from Jamaican or Sumatran tobacco are mildest, with Dominica building up in strength. Honduran and Nicaraguan cigars are weightier and stronger. Havanas, of course, are in a class of their own – imposing in every way.

American cigar aficionados may be denied them (officially), but Havanas are unquestionably the most sought-after cigars in the world.

Cuba is the Mecca of cigar lovers. Though they often extol, and smoke, the premium cigars of Honduras or Nicaragua, or other tobacco-producing countries, cigar lovers regard Havana as their spiritual home.

"The most futile and disastrous day seems well spent when it is reviewed through the blue, fragrant smoke of a Havana Cigar."
EVELYN WAUGH

A cigar taken at La Floridita, one of Ernest Hemingway's favourite bars, is an orgy of smoky nostalgia. A few puffs on a favourite *puro* (as cigars are known in Spain and Latin America), perhaps a Cohiba Lancero, perhaps a Romeo y Julieta Petit Prince, a "snack" cigar evocative of champagne, takes you back to the great days of cigar-smoking.

Each cigar producer has a range of sizes, styles and tastes. These have been refined over the years, just as haute cuisine has changed; the food of our grandmothers evolved into the lighter nouvelle cuisine, but is now claiming back its followers. And so with Havanas. Powerful, sharp, heady flavours were once favoured, only to be superceded by smooth, yet robust, flavours. But the pendulum swings . . .

HEAVENLY HAVANAS

A Havana Alphabet

BOLIVAR: Their Royal Corona is a big smoke, but not overpowering, and is partnered by other lighter tastes. They produce the aptly named Inmensa, a Lonsdale, which is for serious connoisseurs who like a long, almost harsh, smoke.

COHIBA: A recently created family of cigars, dating from 1960, this developed as the personal cigar of Fidel Castro. It was named Cohiba, after the old Spanish word for tobacco. Of their range, the Esplendido (a Churchill) has been compared to a

tenor, the Robusto to a baritone and the Siglo V (a Lonsdale) to a true Havana diva. Which means a well-balanced, spicy aroma.

HOYO DE MONTERREY: A family of cigars for the beginner and the true believer. Their sweet freshness makes them an easy starter, try an Epicure No 2. Hoyo de Monterrey also cater for a robust smoke in the shape of Le Hoyo Des Dieux.

H. UPMANN: This house has been around so long (it was originally a bank) that it is too easily taken for granted. They produced the first Montecristo (named after the fictional Count thereof). They go for big tastes, even risking being on the rough side at times. This is the true Havana taste, never more so than with their Sir Winston (a Churchill, naturally), with its iron hand in a velvet glove taste.

MONTECRISTO: A brand name from 1935, Montecristo cigars took hold of the market only slowly, but are now regarded with almost mystical reverence. The Montecristo A is presented as the emperor of cigars, with rich earthy aromas. A grand classic, often referred to as having ultra-masculine appeal. They also produce, in their wide range, Especiales No 2, which offer a smooth sweetness. The brand took its name from *The Count of Monte Cristo*, the novel by Alexandre Dumas, a favourite story that was read aloud to cigar-rollers as they toiled.

PARTAGAS: A major cigar manufacturer, producing a huge range of premium cigars from the Très Petit Corona to the Double Corona, often referred to as the saint among saints of Havana. Wine terms abound when describing it: full bouquet, ripe fruit, amber flavours, roundness and spicy notes. An exceptional item aimed at connoisseurs.

PUNCH: To quote an authority on Havanas, this brand name is an anagram of all that is Havana – P for princely, U for unique, N for noble, C for charming and H for . . . Havana! All of this family of cigars have strong aromas, often woody, and all are superb. The jewels in their diadem include the Double Coronas, earthy and honeyed, and the Royal Selection, both savoury and spicy, and in the No 12, creamy and floral.

ROMEO Y JULIETA: A favourite house for those who like rich Havanas. Originally famous, or infamous, for its rather harsh cigars made for the English market, it has evolved into a house of distinction. Its stars, introduced only in the 1960s, include the Cazadores, with their spicy and aggressive manner, the Churchills, rich and powerful and the latest Exhibición series, flowery and aromatic to serve the taste of the 1990s.

SAINT LUIS REY: This old house went into decline, but in the 1980s rose again with a well-chosen selection of earthy, spicy flavours, in keeping with the times. Their Prominente, hard to find, has been described as a "little masterpiece". Their whole court of cigars is worth looking out for.

SANCHO PANZA: A very old brand, producing elegant and refined styles, both sweet and aromatic. Their blends are infinitely seductive.

There are of course many other small houses, such as La Flor de Cano, La Gloria Cubano, Rafael Gonzalez, Ramon Allones, El Rey del Mundo . . . all contributing to the glory of the Havana.